MW00737643

Imago, Dei

Elizabeth Johnston Ambrose

Rattle | *Studio City, California* | 2022

Layout and design by Timothy Green

Cover art by Kathryn Clarke Johnston, "The Red Lady"
bassoon-heptagon-khfb.squarespace.com

ISBN: 978-1-931307-50-5

First edition

Rattle Foundation
12411 Ventura Blvd
Studio City, CA 91604
www.rattle.com

CONTENTS

ACKNOWLEDGMENTS

A version of "Father Song" was previously published in *Earth's Daughters,* Fall 2018.

Imago, Dei

i·ma·go

n. pl. **i·ma·goes** or **i·ma·gi·nes** (-g -n z)

1. An insect in its sexually mature adult stage after metamorphosis.
2. *Psychology* An often idealized image of a person, usually a parent, formed in childhood and persisting unconsciously into adulthood.

[Latin im g , im gin-, *image*]

Having been created in the imago Dei, the image of God, all human beings have a God-shaped vacuum built into their hearts. Since nature abhors a vacuum, people keep trying to fill the one inside them.
   —Huston Smith, *"Why Religion Matters"*

Her Father Calls to Explain That Daughters Aren't Easy

*Sons are indeed a heritage of the Lord, and the fruit
of the womb is his reward. As arrows are in the hand
of a mighty man; so are sons of the youth. Happy
is the man that hath his quiver full of them ...*
—Psalm 127:3–5

She was always a disappointment.
Mom said Dad came to the hospital with blue baby sneakers;
on seeing her pink hat through the nursery window,
he trashed them and wept.

Two more girls before Dad got his reward.
It wasn't easy, he tells her. *Three daughters.*
It's Saturday morning. She's hung over
again, watching her daughters from the kitchen window
as they chase cabbage butterflies across the dew-
glittered grass, tennis rackets swinging, blur
of bodies tumbling into each other

and she's thinking of the wild swing of Dad's paddle,
how he chased her sister down the hall
after she wiggled out from where he had pinned
her across his lap, tulip-pink imprint from the first whack
already blooming on Leah's bottom.
He used to say a paddle was less personal;
a hand can get carried away.
But an upcycled cutting board, that's all business.
Spare the rod, spoil the child. And keeping daughters
from spoiling requires a proactive approach.
After all, an ounce of prevention
is worth a pound of cure.

It's like with these moths she's been battling all summer,
seeding marigold and thyme, tying tissue to poles, draping
pantyhose over crowns. Undeterred, they laid their eggs.

[...]

9

So she tried BT, pungent Neem oil, mixed homemade cocktails
of garlic, pepper, and Dawn.
Somewhere along the way she must have screwed up
the recipe: too many cups of this, not enough teaspoons of that.
Lord knows she's never been good at converting
anything, except maybe
marriage into divorce.

Not easy, her father sighs again,
trying to prevent daughters from turning harlots.
He was *just trying to do what the Bible taught was right.*
But, anyway, none of his prophylactics worked.
Neither his belt nor the paddle, nor later,
as they began to fill out and feel out
their dangerous, endangered bodies,
his other tactics:
the picture Bible with its throng of dogs
licking Jezebel's blood, the banned
Cyndi Lauper gloves, forbidden
Daytime soaps, post-date interrogations,
calling them Whore so they could try
on the shame ahead of time.
Still both her sisters got pregnant at nineteen.
For her part, she just spent her twenties letting
lots of men fuck her and her thirties married
to a man who mistook her flailing arms
for worship.

Under the maple, her oldest swats a flicker
of white to the ground, stomps on it.
Through the window she gives her the thumbs-up,
has promised them a quarter a kill. Later,
while they're napping, she'll crouch
over her broccoli, one by one pluck plump
larval bodies from their leafy cradles,
drop and drown them in soapy water.
Sorry, she will say as they sink,
but you're destroying my garden.

She supposes that's how God felt when Eve ate
his apple. How her Dad felt raising daughters.
Now, they have settled into whatever this is.
Across the distance, he is collecting himself as he does,
picking up his conscience like a coat draped across a barstool.
He tells her before hanging up,
I must have done something right.
Look how you turned out.

Ghosts in the Graveyard

There were always more girls at youth group than boys.
Girls are easier to convert. You don't have to convince them
of their worthlessness in the world.
They already know.

Still, boys need saving, too.
Their pastor encouraged the girls to lure their crushes to church.
Before being bathed in the blood of the lamb, he'd been a pimp.
Now he was reborn. From the pulpit of his newest employ, he liked to say:
I've become a different kind of fisher of men.
So they'd bring the boys to Wednesday night youth group,
watch cartoons about blasphemers melting like marshmallows
in a lake of fire. Afterwards, pass a platter of Chips Ahoy,
discuss how to recognize the Whore of Babylon,
take turns guessing which of their classmates were going to hell,

then gather on the church lawn to play Ghosts in the Graveyard.
Under the blinking eyes of the parking lot lights she always pretended
she wasn't fast. She wanted Ricky, so she would let him catch
and pin her against the church's brick façade, his palms pressed
against her panting ribs, his thumbs tempting the band of her bra.
Once, on the way home from a youth group trip to Kings Dominion,
they French-kissed in the bucket of the church van's back seat
while listening to "Sweet Child of Mine" on his Walkman.

Later, Ricky would dump her for Lana, the new girl
who sat in the back pew and whose rich father touched her
where only husbands should. And then Cindy, whose bartender
mother was never home so she got drunk on wine coolers
every Saturday and had already slept with two boys and wept
with relief when she was baptized. A few months later
Ricky dumped Cindy for Misty who showed up at youth group
dark-eyed and haunted but never confessed

who or what had been breaking her.
She must have been the most damaged of all
because it was Misty who Ricky wanted most,

and Misty who finally reeled in Ricky.

Dirty Dancing

Pastor Dave condemned it with a sneer.
Reminded them that lust was a sin, could send them hurtling
straight to hell. But she and Annie snuck into the theater anyway,
afterwards practiced swinging their hips in front of the mirror.
When the local fire hall threw a teen dance,
they swept blue eyeshadow across their lids, Aqua Net-ed
their bangs sky-high, wiggled on polka-dot mini-skirts, piled
jellied bangles from wrist to elbow, drenched
themselves with Love's Baby Soft.
At the dance, Annie waited in the shadows
but *she* wanted to be seen

so when the DJ played "Angel Eyes," she let the
long-haired guy in the skinny jeans and Metallica
muscle shirt lead her into the undulating crowd,
let him swing her Patrick-Swayze-style onto his thigh,
pretended not to feel his manhood straining
against his pants, let him rock her back and forth,
her face pressed into his neck, his greasy stink
of Drakkar and Marlboro Reds.
He was pock-marked and grizzled,
too old to be at a teen dance, and
when he tried to kiss her, she laughed,
pushed him away. He didn't understand,
none of them ever did, how sometimes
good girls just want to feel
dirty,

but a half hour later, when she saw him dirty dancing to "Heaven"
with a dough-faced girl from her biology class,
saw him stick his tongue down her throat,
saw his hands groping the girl's ass
and the girl just letting him, in front of everyone,
she knew then, as she knows even better now:
some have to take what they can get.

Her Father Talks to Her About Sex

If your right hand offends, chop it off,
throw it away. Better for you
to lose one part of yourself than
suffer your whole body to burn.

Throw it away. Better for you
to pluck out your eye. If you don't
suffer, your whole body will burn.
Better to be blind. Better to starve.

Pluck out your eye. If you don't,
think of Eve, naked and ashamed.
Better to be blind. Better to starve
than be exiled from your Father's love.

Think of Eve, naked and ashamed.
Think of your runaway sister, forever
exiled from your father's love.
Think of Delilah. Of Jezebel. Lot's wife.

Think of your runaway sister, forever.
Think of those girls, opening their legs.
Think of Delilah. Of Jezebel. Lot's wife.
Cut off your tongue. Cut out your heart.

Think of those girls, opening their legs.
Suffer. Your whole body burns.
Cut off your tongue. Cut out your heart.
Throw it away. Better for you.

Born Again Virgins

Sunday mornings, she watched them rise
during invocation, heads bowed in shame.
All those girls who had made the mistake
of opening their legs with their hearts.
Deflowered. Who would want them, now

unless they could become virgins again.
The minister waited for them in the baptismal tub like a prom date
and she watched like the girl who hadn't been asked

as he folded them into his embrace,
one palm cupping their reed-like necks,
the other cradling their bellies,
dipped each as in a waltz,
back into the water

One. Two. Three ...

As he held them there, she imagined
the girls' faces as beneath a glass coffin
waiting for their prince's kiss,

or like water lilies that had ripened too soon,
straining for the surface, waiting
for someone to float overhead, reach down,
pluck them from the muck.

Runaway

*During this time the insect is very vulnerable
because it cannot run away.*
—from "What Happens Inside a Cocoon?"

The eighth time Leah ran away, she left bedsheets dangling from the window
like in the movies, though she had actually just walked out the front door.

"Not my good sheets," Mom mourned, lifting them from the mud. Dad called
the police again, rattled off her description. Tangled red hair. Scrawny. Glasses.

You'd think they would have just let her go this time. Been relieved.
She was

eleven the only time she and Leah tried to run away together. Her idea then,
they plotted a map in her Trapper Keeper, threw Cheez Whiz and Saltines

into a blanket knotted like the hobos in Saturday cartoons, stole a five from
mom's purse. First stop: corner 7-Eleven for french fries, two-liter of Coke, box

of matches. Then they humped across the field that stretched beyond their row
of townhouses. It was December in Maryland, sun low in the sky, thin scrape

of frost crunching beneath their Sears Surplus sneakers. They set up camp
behind a silo, huddled in the cold, decided to ration the fries, tried

and failed to light a pile of brown leaves, ketchup packets, and napkins. *I'll keep
trying*, Leah said. She told Leah, *I forgot something. I'll be right back.*

At home, Mom was stirring SpagettiOs on the stove. She set the spoon down,
narrowed her eyes, asked as if she didn't know, *Why on earth would you want to*

runaway is a verb that can also be a noun. Like love. Like wound. Like reject
that narrative. Find, another. Which begs the question: if no one cares to look,

are you still a runaway? The time Leah ruined their mom's sheets, the cops caught her in a D.C. subway station, returned her unshowered and unrepentant.

For years, she remembered it being Dad who took Leah's bedroom away, made her sleep in the hall closet until she graduated. It was actually Mom.

After graduation, Leah took off for the Navy; this time no one tried to stop her. *She was someone else's problem now*, her dad said, as if daughters come with

an expiration date. For her own part, she stuck it out another year. She'd never been good at running away. Ask her mother. Ask the boyfriend her first year of

community college that practiced his boxing moves on her. Ask her father. When he saw her black eye, he shrugged: *If you stay, what can you expect?*

When he dumped her for another girl, she finally left, drove cross-country, 2,000 miles of Counting Crows' *rolling a new life over, turning the girl into*

the ground. She has since read that certain caterpillars, the kind that become the moths people mistake for hummingbirds, bury their cocoons in graves.

Back home, there was a third sister. Six years younger.
In all these memories, where did she go?

Degenerate

In a number of species of moths the mouthparts
are all degenerate in the imagos
—Gordon Ramel, Lepidoptera 101

Her mother loved the Ellen DeGeneres show. *Ellen Degenerate,* her dad scoffed, switching the channel. *Ron,* her mother would say. Just like that, *Ron.* The way you protest when you're not sure you're right. He didn't know yet that her youngest sister had come out. *Don't tell your father,* mom made her promise. So many secrets. Sometimes she wished she was Catholic so at least someone could hear her confess, so she could stop grinding her teeth against the stones collecting in her mouth. So she could discover if she actually did have a mouth.

Once a lesbian came to church, huddled in the pew behind her. She knew she was a lesbian by her hair, and also because she could hear her crying when the pastor said abstinence was not enough. You had to not want the thing you wanted. You had to cut off all the desiring parts, become an amputee. The lesbian never came back to church. Later, confused by science class, she brought this up with her pastor, *But I didn't think God could make a mistake?*

Her pastor smiled. *He doesn't. He makes tests.*

How a Caterpillar Turns into a Butterfly

*First, the caterpillar digests itself, releasing enzymes
to dissolve all of its tissues. If you were to cut open
a cocoon or chrysalis at just the right time, caterpillar
soup would ooze out.*
        *—from "How Does a Caterpillar Turn into
        a Butterfly?"*

She doesn't know for certain that it hurts,
but speaking from experience, she imagines
that it does.

Tristesse

Crying after sex isn't sexy. She tried not to do it, pressed her face to her pillow
so they wouldn't see. But it happened. Every. Damned. Time.

She wondered if each went home, told his roommates about the girl at the club:
thigh-high boots, leather skirt, how she pulled him out to the dance floor, sweat

slick, or slipped her arm through his, led him to the bar, practically drank him
under the table, how at last call she reached into his pocket, found his cigarettes,

his keys, asked: *Where's your car?* At her place, like something out of a porno,
how she pushed him onto the bed, climbed on top, began bucking and moaning

so loud her roommate banged on the door, yelled for her to *shut the fuck up*,
but she just threw her head back, howling like something hungry and loosed.

Then, after all that show, burst into tears.

The less experienced ones tried to comfort her, awkwardly patted her arm
while reaching for their pants; the others just made for the door.

Later, after she was married, she would hear Oprah call this *postcoital tristesse*.
Post-sex blues. Like a Crayola shade. Like a Sherwin-Williams palette.

But if she was a color,
it was the ring of scum in a draining
sink, the smudge of an overzealous eraser,
water in a vase of rotting stems, the hungry
pit of a disinterested yawn, of skin snagged
in a zipper, the smear of moths
dragged across a windshield,

the color of a gate shutting,
a psalm book, closing.

Apology

I guess it's my fault, her Dad admitted once.
The reason you girls are all screwed up about men.
She had just graduated college, was home for the summer before starting
a fellowship, straddling him as he lay stomach down on the floor.
She pressed her wrists together, butterflied her palms across his spine,
waited for him to exhale,
then threw her weight forward.
He grunted as his back cracked under her hands.

It's fine, she said. *We're fine.*

Encounter

*In the aha experience that characterizes the mirror stage,
the infant grasps the connection between the image and
its own existence. The infant experiences the imago as
... a meaningful form. It is important to note that the
imago is external to the infant. The 'I' comes into being
not as an emanation of the individual, but as the result
of an encounter with an other.*
  —"Imago"

In grad school, she studied Lacan's mirror stage:
the moment the infant recognizes her image as other
and ever after feels divided from her self.
She used this theory to explain to her boyfriend
why she was such a crappy girlfriend:
I am pursuing lack, she offered.
He was a man in med school
so didn't understand how a body
that appears perfectly whole
can be a hole
unless in the moment
a hole
was wholly what he wanted.

Father Song

There is one particular sort of tissue that remains: in a number of places in the insect's body are collections of special formative cells, which ... have stayed hidden or protected during this partial death. Each of these groups of cells is called an imaginal bud ...
—*"What Happens Inside a Cocoon"*

Imagine one version is simply refrain:
how he missed
> open house and plays,
> birthdays and prom,
> but never the chance
> to point out her flat chest,
> her crooked teeth. All
> she couldn't get right.
Song she can't brace herself against.
Going about her day and suddenly
the snaking contours of its chorus
uncoiling, rising up, swelling into bombast
like that time in the kitchen he was throwing
cans and words that dented walls and floors.
And other things.

There are other versions.
Like the one where her dog dies and he holds her face to his chest.
Or the time her fever spikes and he lays his palm on her cheek.
Or when he is tickling her on the living room floor, and she's giggling,
Daddy, Daddy. Stop.
And hoping he never does.

There's the version where she is impervious,
where skipping stones don't sink,
and the version where she forgives him
because every girl needs a dad

and, anyway, every song's an echo:
she reminds herself he had no father
just some guy named Red who stole him one summer,
made him his side-kick speeding through states
until the leaves turned and he dropped her father
on her grandmother's step like returned mail.

The version she hums to herself when she's rocking her babies is this:
after her divorce, he sends her a Fender,
a cheap flea-market find. Around its neck he has bound
a familiar gold-flecked strap and she remembers being seven,
awake past bedtime, drawn like a moth
to the light of his bedroom, pressing her body
against the sliver of his door.
He was sitting on the bed, cradling a guitar,
around its neck that same strap.
In this version his voice is soft,
his fingers gently pluck the strings.

Imagine he is writing a love song.
Memorize every word.

Her Sister's Demons

She invites her sister for the holiday
but Leah wants to bring her demons,
says they can play with hers,
says they're better trained since last time,
haven't had an accident in months.
Leah's even taught them tricks:
Lay down. Play dead.
At night they sleep in a crate.

Still, she worries.
She's kept hers small, trained
them to be satisfied with scraps,
not to beg. To leave it.

Not her sister.
Leah's been feeding them right from the table,
letting them lick her plate, sometimes
getting down on all fours
to suckle them herself.

Now Leah tells her: they're a package deal.
No demons, no sister.

But she knows what will happen.
It will be just like last time.

They'll gate them in the back,
and she'll start to help her sister unpack.
It won't take long before Leah's demons charge
right through the invisible fence,
and right on their heels, her own little imps.
The lot of them loose and howling like a god-
damn pack of feral strays.

They'll tear through her cul-de-sac,
dig holes in garden beds, nose through garbage.
Terrorize small children.
When at last they slink home,
mud-slimed, stinking of shit,
some still-warm victim dangling
from one of their red-frothed maws
it will take her hours to scrub them clean.
She'll be making apologies for days.
Her husband won't be happy.

She tries to explain this to her sister
what could happen if they get loose.

Don't be silly, Leah assures her.
*I've been letting them run free all these years
and, see?*

They always come home to eat.
They know the hand that feeds them.

Her Father Calls to Tell Her
He Misses Their Mother

He could never control his temper, so
when the car slammed into them from behind,
even though no one was hurt,
even though Mom grabbed his arm,
begged him, her voice like water over a wound,
he shrugged her off, flung open his door, hurtled
from the car, cursing.

She and her sisters crouched in the backseat,
watching through the rear window.
He was scariest when crossed, rage an ignited fuse
threading up his neck to his ears.

The other driver hit the gas, but Dad lunged,
grabbed the door, held on as the car pulled
away. Their mother screamed *let go*
but he wouldn't, so they all watched as his legs
collapsed, as his knees dragged, as one arm fell,
scraping road. When finally the car threw him,
he rolled to a stop in a cloud of dust and exhaust,
lay crumpled on the road,
like something broken,
for a very long time.

Later, she and Leah huddled outside
their parents' bathroom, watched Mom hover
over him with her tweezers, picking gravel
like shrapnel from his skin.
You should have let go, she said, her face tight.

Thirty years later, Mom has finally moved out,
bought a condo, an aquarium, lives alone with her fish.
Saturday mornings, he calls his oldest daughter,
voice full of gravel. *Was it really that bad?*

Dad, she keeps saying, *you have to let go.*

Parasite

*During all of this, the caterpillar, which grows more
and more bloated as the larvae mature, isn't yet
showing any signs of being manipulated. Incredibly,
you can't even tell it's behaving any differently,
even as it swells to the point where it looks like it's
going to burst.*
—from "Absurd Creature of the Week,"
Wired Magazine

There is a species of wasp that can inject up to eighty eggs into the body
of a caterpillar. When the eggs hatch, the larvae stay safely buried in their
host's warm body, feeding on it from within until they mature and chew
their way out. Brainwashed by its parasite, the caterpillar guards the
larvae like its own while they continue to feed. The doomed creature even
helps the enemy's larva spin their own cocoon, lending them its own silk.

When she finds one of these parasitized caterpillars on her plants, she calls
her husband to witness. *See,* her husband says, *this proves there is no God.
What kind of God would design such torment?* She still hasn't found a way
to explain to him those years she lived bloated with shame, or even now
her desire to protect the thing that fed on her.

Her Father Calls to Tell Her She Should Stop Writing About American Women

She is bathing her two-year-old, so has to cradle
the phone between her ear and neck.
You don't know how good you have it, he tells her.
Write about women over there,
the ones in veils,
the ones they hang,
the girls they cut with stones.
Do you understand? Do you see what I mean?

but she sees her daughter
clambering out of the tub,
dripping and pink, giggling
I'm naked! I'm naked!
She toddles drunkenly down the hall,
in her bedroom drops to the floor,
tugs on rainboots,
begins to explore the space between her legs.
Finding pleasure, she looks up at her mother, beams
as if to say: Isn't this wonderful?
And all my own?

Do you understand?

Rapture

At the first news of pandemic,
thinking this might really be the end.
Finally.
And in that moment feeling like a fish released from rough
and awkward hands, arcing into the silk
envelope of a stream

weightless.

Like when she's been dancing, spinning in heated centrifuge
until the body's layers separate,
ripple out from the center

or after the three Manhattans it's taken to strip
the thick veneer of surface, let it slip and puddle
at her ankles.

But all that relief short-lived

more like after the water's skin
accepts the penny thrown at it, slight
disturbance, momentary flutter
then still again

every wish swallowed

because although she tried
she could never shed the inherited
corpse, the sarcophagus of heavy flesh and bone,
couldn't unzip herself from its thick-walled tenement, abandon
it drowned at the bottom of some baptismal tub.
Maybe the pastor should have held her under longer.

Maybe the problem is she has been all surface,
sins that should have weighted her like stones
instead keeping her afloat.

Surfeit of nothing.

The anchoring paradox:
At once all body
and nobody

because whether you starve it
or pour all manner of things into it

you still have to believe a body matters
that its weight on this earth is worth
inhabiting,

even when the earth itself isn't worth inhabiting
because it's going to fall away soon, too.
Why invest, why try
when you grow up expecting the end times any day?
All those days she came home from school to an empty
house, neighbors not answering her knock, no one
picking up the phone,
she convinced herself all the good people had been raptured,
lifted like air.

And her?

Left behind
weighted to the earth
because she was never any good
at being good.

So when her mom walked through the door
balancing groceries on her hip and the neighbor's Chevy
growled into their drive and the phone vibrated

[...]

against the wall, a boy calling, she resolved to be better

one way or another
to weigh less.

The Ten Commandments of Loving
a Recovering Evangelical

Don't mistake her as easy.
She's spent her life on her knees
slaking her thirst, thimble by thimble.
Her degenerate mouth is dry of divine.
Which means you'll do.

Don't try to compete
with her alpha O mega flesh-
made-word-made-flesh again.
A little death's a little death and, anyway,
He'll always talk a better game.
He's been wooing her since the womb

which you should understand
she's still trying to understand

as/is
part/all
of/her

but

always/never/should be

&

never/definitely/in certain cases

yours

which is also to say, before you undress her
acknowledge her Daddy
issues are no joke

[…]

(A God, a Son, and a Holy Spirit
walk into a bar and ask for a Virgin Mary.
The bartender says:
Get a womb.)

Take seriously her wicked
sense of humor, whittled while waiting
on the receiving end of the Good
Word's punch
line. And because she's spent
an eternity waiting to be
plucked

she's going to be all kinds
of mixed up about your rose petal
candlelit bubble bath fantasy
(how long in that tub
how long drowning)

You'll have to learn
to speak in tongues, carnal
communion she's (c)literally craving
since that sunrise service when she hurled
her hysteric hymn-sung hymn-singed
self into the aisle, hollow & hollering
entermesavemeannihilatemeremakeme
baby o baby o baby
because it's all about the milk & honey,
honey

Now steel yourself. The taste
of iron sharpens iron
and hers is the strength
of a lifetime of stonings

So if her three-bourbons-in-fire-
        and-brimstone-filled-to-the-brim-
kind-of-crazy-cunning-lingual

love scares you,
make no idol threats.

I told you already:
One distant deity is as good as another.

This was never about you.

Is a butterfly's life any better than a caterpillar's? Was all that suffering in the cocoon worth it? Is a volcano happier after it erupts? These are children's questions. It doesn't even make sense to ask. The bug has no choice. The cocoon is forced upon it. And then nature runs its course.

—Sam Anderson, "The Truth about Cocoons," New York Times

CITED MATERIAL

Butterfly image from *The Book of Vegetables*, Alan French, 1907.

"How Does a Caterpillar Turn into a Butterfly?" *Scientific American* 10 Aug. 2012. <scientificamerican.com>

"Imago," from "Lacan: The Mirror Stage," *Critalink*, Dept. of English, University of Hawaii. <english.hawaii.edu>

Simon, Matt. "Absurd Creature of the Week," *Wired* 17 Oct. 2014. <wired.com>

Smith, Huston. *Why Religion Matters: The Fate of the Human Spirit in an Age of Disbelief,* Harper Collins, 2001.

"What Happens Inside a Cocoon?" *Lost in Science* 12 Feb. 2011 <lostinscience.wordpress.com>

Ramel, Gordon. "Lepidoptera 101: Much Loved Order of the Moths and Butterflies," *Earth Life.* <earthlife.net>

ABOUT THE RATTLE CHAPBOOK SERIES

The Rattle Chapbook Series publishes and distributes a chapbook to all of *Rattle*'s print subscribers along with each quarterly issue of the magazine. Most selections are made through the annual Rattle Chapbook Prize competition (deadline: January 15th). For more information, and to order other chapbooks from the series, visit our website.

www.Rattle.com/chapbooks